THE ART OF

Bitchcraft

GU█████ ᴛO THE ᴍAGIC OF *GETTING WHAT YOU WANT*

KAARONICA EVANS-WARE

SOURCEBOOKS, INC.®
NAPERVILLE, ILLINOIS

Published by Sourcebooks, Inc.
P.O. Box 4410, Naperville, Illinois 60567-4410
(630) 961-3900
Fax: (630) 961-2168
www.sourcebooks.com

Library of Congress Cataloging-in-Publication Data

Evans-Ware, Kaaronica.
  The art of bitchcraft : the thinking woman's tell-all guidebook to
the art of being a bitch / Kaaronica Evans-Ware.
      p. cm.
   ISBN-13: 978-1-4022-0881-2
   ISBN-10: 1-4022-0881-2
   1. Women—Psychology. 2. Assertiveness in women. 3. Women—
Attitudes. I. Title.

HQ1206.E934 2007
155.3'33—dc22

2006100790

Printed and bound in the United Staes of America
VP   10 9 8 7 6 5 4 3 2 1

Dedication

For my parents, Andrew and Judith, with understanding, respect, and profound love. For my husband, Butch, who is man enough to love a Queen Bee.

Acknowledgments

This book would not have been possible without God to whom I pray faithfully and diligently. I offer earthly thanks to many people, starting with my bestfriend and fellow writer Lawana Holland-Moore who called the first day of 2005 with the inspiration I needed to start this book. I would like to concoct a cauldron full of thanks to: my editor, Deborah Werksman, whose finely-tuned bitch vibes zeroed in on my manuscript and whose artistic bitchery is changing publishing one book at a time; my agent, Melissa Flashman, for her enthusiastic support of Enlightened Bitchcraft and for being a top-notch bitch doctor; my children Samonia, Shamarra, Ismail'ila and Rabi'a; my family in Decatur, especially Judy Evans, Andrew Evans, Kyra Evans, Kofi Houston, DeAndre Harper, Kay Alcorn, Chikada Long, Vivienne Evans, and Matt Morgret for reacting with shock and then laughter upon learning of my latest book project; my family and friends who've nurtured the writer in me in many ways, Tamika Ware, Delonté Moore, Martin Proctor, Jessica Leerhoff Young, Brian Holmes, Sonia Hayward, Elmyra Manigault, Tia Kelley, Venise Berry, Tananarive Due, Ahmad Wright, Sungee Jones, Sandra Nelson, Theresa Ford, Tiffany Belk, Elaine Evans, Dr. Luther Adams, Bonni Hamilton, Dawn Frederick, Beatrice McFadden, Barbara Myers, C.C. Crispo, Tressia Amacher, Lisa Shea, Karen Johnson, Teketha Bond, Jae Bryson, Dia Satori, The Loft Literary Center, William Schafer, Fred Shafer and others who shall remain nameless, but you know who you are, for your artistic encouragement over the years; and a special thanks to my dear husband, Rudolph "Butch" Ware, who first accused me of practicing Bitchcraft and for keeping my sense of humor fresh.

Contents

When a man gives his opinion he's a man. When a woman gives her opinion she's a bitch.

—*Bette Davis*

Introduction

> It is good to have an end to journey toward, but it is the journey that matters in the end.
>
> **—Ursula K. Le Guin**

Have you suffered accusations of being "difficult" lately? How about being "unpleasant"? And have you been those things? Chances are you've just been making sure the world meets your high standards.

This book will introduce you to the enlightened practice of Bitchcraft and will liberate those of you who've suppressed your true selves. This is the thinking woman's tell-all guidebook to the art of being a bitch. The word bitch has negative connotations, but it's most often used when women are being aggressive, ambitious, and tough. I encourage you to embrace these attributes and claim, study, and develop your bitchiness. It's time for strong women all over the world to discover the true characteristics of the hidden craft we've been unwittingly practicing for years. You will then be ready to enhance your innate but undeveloped bitchiness on your way to becoming a real Queen Bee.

Major subjects I'm going to introduce to you include: how to use Bitchcraft in the real world, how to form a bitch's coven, and how to repel the dark side of Bitchcraft to ensure a blissful life. I will also address how to deal with bitch hunts, bitch trials, bitch-induced mass hysteria, and accusations of bitcheresy. Such persecutions arise due to the actions of unenlightened bitches, those who wickedly harm others or have completely devoted themselves to the dark side of the craft. This book is the manual for the enlightened bitch—the Bitchcraft Book of Light and Shadows, if you will, direly needed for the survival of bitches and our craft.

THE ART OF

Bitchcraft

I'm tough, I'm ambitious,
and I know exactly what
I want. If that makes me
a bitch, okay.

—*Madonna*

1

THE TRUTH ABOUT BITCHES AND THEIR CRAFT

Raise your glasses ladies. It's time for a toast. First to Madonna for telling it like it is. Hear! Hear! Now to ourselves for accepting the obvious and finally listening to what people have been telling us for years. By buying this book, dear reader, you've taken the first step down the road to owning your bitchiness. In spite of what we've been told, being a bitch isn't all that bad. Whether we like it or not, it has become abundantly clear over the years that we can't change how we are anyway. So why not embrace the bitch within with open arms? So what if we have complicated, demanding personalities? When did that become a crime? If the world wants to call us bitches for standing up, asserting ourselves, and going after what we want, then so be it; be a bitch and be proud of it!

The word bitch is often used to degrade women who act in ways some don't think we should. All it really means to be a bitch is to be independent, persistent, ambitious, confident, determined, self-satisfied, strong-willed, tenacious, and undaunted. In short, bitches are complex.

We notice the bitch right away. Her carriage is more self-assured than most. Her stride says "I know who I am and I know where I'm going" with every step. Let us pause to consider the striking profile of our striding bitch! Conjure an image of her in your mind. Her gait is not a sashay; she does not wish to draw attention to her feminine wiles, powerful though they may be. She walks with poise and purpose, her head held high. Her steely eyes do not wander from irrelevant face to irrelevant face; they remained fixed forward. See through those eyes. She could not care less if people think she's a bitch. She's a queen among commoners and she knows it. A regal bitch is far too independent to let society dictate who she is. You too can be a regal bitch.

The truth about bitches is that we aren't born—we're made. We aren't forged in the smoldering bowels of an infernal laboratory, as some would have us believe, unless this man's world is such a laboratory! We enter the world as women, like any others. The breathtaking implication of this simple truth is that all women have the innate potential to become powerful, feared, and respected bitches. Those of us who grow up to be bitches cannot suppress the inner rebellion that ferments when we are repeatedly told to stay in our place. We sense our inner power at an early age and begin channeling our unruliness.

Without knowing it, or claiming it, we begin to bitch.

Up to this point in our history, bitches have been made accidentally and circumstantially, out of sheer necessity alone. By walking this road with me, my bitchlings, you are opening yourself to the possibility of mapping uncharted terrain in the history of Bitchcraft. Together we will bring Bitchcraft out of obscurity and misunderstanding and take it to a whole new level. Cling tight to your bitch-brooms and fly with me to new heights!

Wonderful women renowned for their peace-loving natures are unwittingly made into bitches every day when they feel the need to speak up for themselves, confront tough issues, or enforce their high standards. We applaud such women for standing up, but because they do not name their refusal they cannot embrace it; their resistance can only be partial and contingent. They only rarely become truly radical bitches. They bitch today and wilt tomorrow. Because of the degrading intentions behind the name, most of us have feared to drink too deeply from our bitch's cauldron. When we press the limits and are called a bitch, we shrink from the charge. Sometimes we find the courage to stand, but then finding ourselves standing alone, we falter. But herein lies the hope for our liberation. We shall name and own our bitchery and overcome our fear of our fellow bitches to stand together in radical bitchdom.

In the preceding paragraph, I made a conscious parallel between witchcraft and the art of being a bitch. Like witches, bitches possess awesome powers that inspire fear and resentment. But there are important differences. A witch purposefully practices a craft and a bitch is loath to have hers identified. We bitches certainly do not put in the time honing our craft that witches do honing theirs. Witches know what they are doing, while we artisans remain totally oblivious.

It is time we took a long, hard look at ourselves and remove the cloak of ignorance. Once we do, we realize that every time we say "no" in the face of gender-specified conformity, we are, in fact, practicing a time-honored but misunderstood craft. Why do you think complaining is often referred to in our society as "bitching"? Whenever we take it upon ourselves to fight the hard fight, we are unwitting artisans. Bitchcraft is a skill that may change your life, but in order for that to happen, we must prevail against the paralyzing ignorance and accept the fact that it exists. That is one of the major goals of this short book, this bitch's creed. The importance of this act of uncovering Bitchcraft is simple: if we continue to let our craft go unknown and unnamed, then we relegate future generations of bitches to slog in obscurity and isolation, one of the greatest enemies of enlightened bitchdom.

bitchery \bi-chə-rē\ n : A process of focused will, passion, and energy to effect change in yourself, your environment, and around the world.

Awakening the Bitch

The first step in our re-education is to awaken the sleeping bitch within. As the dawn of our bitch self-light breaks, we begin to rub the crust from our eyes and see clearly—maybe for the first time.

We start to see others, ourselves, our lives, our jobs, etc. for what they really are and we don't like what we've become. Here are some undeniable signs that the bitch in us has awakened and that we've tapped into her vibrations:

- We want to make a change.
- We focus on that desire and act upon it without seeking outside approval.
- Our actions make the people around us uncomfortable, confused, and nervous. Yet, we don't care.
- Our indifference sparks the formation of posses. A bitch hunt is imminent. We still don't care.
- We are impervious in our quest for self-actualization. As we begin to know ourselves, we begin to like ourselves more every day, even if no one likes the fact that we've called our sleeping bitch into action. We decide that's their problem. We may even tell them so.
- An alert is released to the general public, the usual consequence of bitch-induced mass hysteria. We remain calm knowing that we are the eye of the storm.
- The accusations mount. Secret depositions are recorded. A bitch trial is around the corner. We go out and buy a snazzy new suit for the occasion.

Persecution of the Bitch

As we begin the metamorphosis from ignorance to awakening, we may face persecution. We will soon find out, as all bitches have, that it's lonely at the top. Do not let this sway you. If a mob of angry townsfolk starts gathering torches to conduct a bitch hunt, do not falter. Stay strong. Protect the life of your complex spirit. We can take this as an opportunity to strive towards a stronger sense of self. Whatever Bitchcraft trials the mob might stage are occasions for us to get stronger; apparent obstacles like these are, in reality, only steps on the path to mastering our craft.

The Troglodyte

If we take the persecution personally we will be giving in to the major force that has kept bitches down over the centuries. This bitch-hunting—which is all too real—breaks many a bitch. It forces her to deny, dissemble, and in the end disfigure her talents.

bitch-induced mass hysteria: a condition in which a large group of people exhibit extreme anxiety or a set of panic-like symptoms, for which there is no physical explanation, as a reaction to a skillful Bitchcraft artisan. It can also be a result of negative, war-like Bitchcraft.

bitch hunt \'bich 'hunt'\ n:
A social campaign launched against strong, ambitious, tenacious, aggressive, and revolutionary women on the pretext of investigating social misdeeds. Used as a cover to harass and undermine women with differing views. If successful, death of spirit, ambition, and sense of self is imminent.

In the face of persecution, unwitting—and therefore unwilling—bitches hide their gifts and practice their still unnamed craft only in isolation. Hiding in the caves to avoid defamation, these bitches poison their own cauldrons by isolating themselves and accepting the shame cast upon them.

These troglodyte bitches—and most of us have been this and nothing more until now—are a tragic waste of potential. Still worse, they are a curse to their enlightened bitch sisters. Powerful magic, worked only in isolation and shame, can only be self-serving and negative. The troglodyte bitch works the dark side of the force. In order to come into the light she must decide to leave her cave days behind her.

Banish Self-doubt

In order to come into the light, we must have the confidence not to shrink at the moment of persecution. Without confidence we fall prey to all sorts of ills that are so destructive even the most renowned bitch doctor hasn't discovered the batch of spells strong enough to banish this self-doubt. Until now, that is.

bitch trial \bich'tri'əl\ n:
An informal social examination before an incompetent, often frightened and jealous court of "peers." It is also a test of devotion, patience, and stamina through arduous periods of suffering or persuasion.

Eleanor Roosevelt once said, "You gain strength, courage, and confidence by every experience in which you really stop to look fear in the face. You are able to say to yourself, 'I have lived through this horror. I can take the next thing that comes along.' You must do the thing you think you cannot do."

Ladies, self-doubt has destroyed many a great bitch. It's powerful. Don't become a statistic. If we are to overcome it, we mustn't make the rookie mistake of calling ourselves bitches and failing to have a ready collection of bitch spells to keep us soaring in spite of the angry mob pulling us down by the cape.

Spells are ideal for facing our fears of possible reproach from these less-advanced troglodyte bitches that are trapped in the cave. It's smart to acknowledge their existence since their strength is undeniable. Their eyes are like x-ray machines. Their dark bitch vibes radiate from them and almost knock us down off our brooms, but we shouldn't overly concern ourselves with this. As long as we are genuine in our quest for personal truth and self-actualization, things like worrying about what others will think of us begin to matter less and less.

grimoire \grim•wär\ n: Highly secret book of rituals, affirmations, training techniques, guidelines, procedures, and declarations of bylaws written with the bitch or coven in mind. Only another enlightened bitch can see your book of lights and shadows.

Once you've become self-actualized, you can start a coven and come back for some of the first stage bitches. Until then, you can't let them hold you back. Good intentions will get us to the path, but we have to conjure up something really special if we want to master the art of Bitchcraft. Here are a few powerful incantations. Jot them down in your grimoire.

- It's okay to be a bitch because a bitch to me means…
- I will not fear bitch hunts. I will view them as signs of my success along the path of enlightenment.
- I will love the bitch in me. She keeps me real.
- I will let my bitch self sleep, but never die.

Remember, self-doubt stops us from standing firm in who we really are. It keeps us from addressing the issues that matter to us. Each one of us has something unique and amazing within us, but when we fail to see that, we stunt our spiritual growth. Unless and until we take the time to discover what that unique thing is, we will always have self-doubt.

Shame & the Bitch

I can't stress enough the gravity of the shame many of us feel upon using our craft. When the irresistible urge to bitch presents itself and we succumb, it is only too natural to feel like we've done something wrong. We're afraid we have shamed ourselves, our parents, children, and partners, so we feel terrible. When we see the look of shock and embarrassment on our loved one's faces, we often ask ourselves one of two questions: "What the heck is the matter with me?" or "Why can't I act right?" Suddenly, we begin to suppress our ideals because they are objectionable or "bitchy." We wallow in shame instead of banishing it and now we find we have inadvertently made a pact to censor ourselves in the event of future urges. This is a mistake and here's why. The shame shouldn't be for being a bitch. The only shame we should feel is when we use our powers for evil rather than good. If we're bitching because we want to selfishly control others or cause harm, then we are back in the cave and merit censure. But if we're bitching because something is just dead wrong, or somebody is relieving themselves on our heads and calling it rain, then why should we be ashamed?

Unwarranted censorship is in direct violation of bitch law, which clearly dictates that we tell it like it is. If we don't make the distinction, we bottle up the good with the bad and eventually we explode in an outburst of random bitchery. To bitch hunters these outbursts often look like fits, convulsions, and spasms. To an enlightened Bitchcraft practitioner, they are simply a matter of bad alchemy. When the positive and negative humors co-mingle and thrive indiscriminately in the body of a bitch, such outbursts are inevitable.

Random acts of bitchiness are clear marks of a bitch that hasn't dealt with the shame she may feel for being a social outcast. Therefore, the sanctity of the craft is threatened. Any future attempts to assemble together in a united front of sisterhood are difficult. So, we have to be careful not to upset the delicate balance of proper Bitchcraft.

A nice, well-mannered lady got fed-up one day. Her "speech"—confrontations, demands, and outburst of bitchiness—startled everyone. Soon, ladies everywhere got fed-up, too. Society could determine only one cause: Bitchcraft.

BITCHCRAFT 101: HONE YOUR CRAFT

Once the search for the true bitch in you begins and you start down the path to a better you, it is easy to become intimidated or nervous. Such feelings are normal, but don't let them paralyze you. Few things are as tragic as a quivering, hesitant bitchling! These constraining feelings are, for bitches, not unlike the shackles that have imprisoned witches for centuries. This chapter will provide us with the keys necessary to free the enlightened bitch within each of us. We will learn about the four elements of Bitchcraft, along with the fundamentals of keeping a grimoire. We will also learn powerful bitch spells—positive affirmations that promise to liberate us from the prison walls of unreflective reluctance. Only then can we move beyond the confining darkness of the cave and wield the shining torch of our enlightened craft.

The Four Elements

In essence, Bitchcraft is composed of managing four basic elements: awakening, persecution, self-doubt, and shame. In order to become transformed artisans, we must awaken our bitch self and grasp her power, overcome the fear of persecution we are sure to face, banish all self-doubt no matter how paralyzing, and overcome the shame we feel when we utilize our art form. Only then will we become the physical embodiment of enlightened Bitchcraft.

Element #1: Awakening

A woman's intellect and intuition can be powerful tools if honed properly. That sixth sense we feel deep within us shouldn't be ignored. In some situations it is all that we have. The ability to tap into this vast reservoir of feeling is what separates the masters of the craft from the beginners. Centering our minds is vital to the survival of the craft. Think about it. How many stressed out, unfocused troglodytes have you come across in your life? How about within the last year? The last month? The last hour? Most bitches are extremely passionate people. Our emotions can run high and the next thing we know we are casting misdirected bitch spells and wreaking havoc on the world.

To avoid such tribulations, we have to be willing to see things for what they really are. There will be trying times after you've opened your mind and spirit and are soaring high, free from the worries of regular, everyday bitches. When they swoop down upon you—and they will—recall the reason you started this journey to keep it all in perspective.

Awakening Pledge

I pledge to provoke the sleeping bitch within.
I pledge to always see others as they present themselves and not how I wish them to be.
I pledge to toughen my mind against false accusations.
I pledge to use original and independent thinking.

Element #2: Persecution

Words have the power to uplift or tear down. The unenlightened world fights hard to use our mastery of the art form against us. They will defame our character and use tones designed to break our spirit. Don't give in to the power trips. Your words have great power, too. Use them wisely. When you are an enlightened bitch, you will speak your mind, but you will also take the time to weigh your words and use them effectively.

Anti-persecution Pledge

I pledge to put my accusers in the hot seat and demand proof of all allegations.
I pledge to ignore the panic others feel when faced with my enlightened bitchery.
I pledge to continuously challenge and rethink traditional assumptions.
I pledge to persuade without antagonizing.

Element #3: Self-Doubt

To banish self-doubt you must acknowledge how often you experience it. Only then can you clearly see what it is doing to your mind, body, and spirit. Don't worry if, at first, these backward thoughts are all you have! Like a witch perfecting her spell, the key to believing in yourself is through consistent self-reflection. Here are some key points to remember:

- Follow every negative thought with a positive one.
- Thoroughly think about it before you speak about it.
- Try not to take everything personally.

The point here is that we are always creating our worlds with our minds. Every day, every hour, every minute, and every second, whether we realize it or not, something we are thinking or feeling develops into our reality. Thoughts are powerful—use them wisely. Keep your bitchery firm but balanced.

Banish Self-doubt Pledge

I pledge to be honest about my need for change.
I pledge to seek my own approval.
I pledge to respect the individuality of my thoughts.
I pledge to bolster my confidence with each trial.

Element #4: Shame

You will undoubtedly feel shame once you start to utilize your art. This is a trick! When most of us picture the image of a bitch, we see a disheveled, loud, obnoxious, uncouth woman who shouts obscenities at everyone, including humpback ladies and wobbly-knee toddlers.

This is not the physical embodiment of the true bitch, the real bitch, the enlightened bitch. Such bitches we see running households or empires. Their spines are erect and their heads are held high.

Anti-Shame Pledge

I pledge to always think rationally while honoring
my emotions.
I pledge to avoid overreacting.
I pledge to cleanse my Bitchdom of shame.
I pledge to handle disappointment with grace.

The Grimoire

A grimoire is a cherished, hand-written book of guidelines, techniques, historical accounts of important bitchery, and just about anything that can and has helped bitches on the path toward enlightenment.

What you put into your grimoire is entirely up to you. We hold the key to freeing the masterful artisan that lies dormant in each of us. By using our grimoire, our handbook of light and dark bitchiness, to record our good and bad deeds, we will soon reveal a more effective bitch.

Before we get into the fundamentals of starting and keeping a grimoire, we need to go over some key rules first:

✭ To prevent it from falling into the wrong hands and being used against us, our grimoires must be kept hidden. They contain all the secrets to our success, but also a catalog of our weaknesses.

* Share your grimoire with no one unless she is a fellow and trusted bitch.
* Preserve it. Take care of it.
* Write in it every day.
* Create a book that really reflects who you are and where you are going within the realm of Bitchcraft.

Grimoire Fundamentals

1. Now, the first thing you must do is title your grimoire. Use your bitch vibes to select the perfect title. Here are a few examples on how to title your grimoire:

The Secret Grimoire of [your name]
[your name] Book of Light and Shadows
The Key of [your name]
[your name] Book of Philosophy
The Greater Key of [your name], the Queen Bee, the Sweet Pea, or the Wannabe

2. Then date your grimoire. Dates are important. As you begin your soul search, you'll want to know the day you start changing the quality of your bitchiness. If you plan to record in your grimoire regularly, you may want to establish a volume number with each new grimoire you begin.

3. Now, on the very first page, record your mission for the growth of your complex spirit. Since this will likely be your first grimoire, start out with a goal that's not intimidating. Examples might be: accepting your demanding personality, or awakening the bitch within. Whatever you chose for your mission, make it good.

4. Organize the various sections of your grimoire. Here are a few suggested sections:

✮ Goals and Aspirations
Write down your short-term and long-term goals. Now, write down any aspirations (spiritual or otherwise) and what you know you need to work on. If there is any bitch out there whose characteristics you admire, place her name and her attributes here. Then make an outline of your plan of action. Make note of the date you start. All of this will help you figure out what you need to achieve and when. This is a great subject to have in your grimoire as it helps us to learn more about ourselves, and much less importantly, others.

✮ Dreams
Many messages are conveyed to us through our dreams. We receive warnings and answers to perplexing questions. In this section you can jot down your interpretations and any personal ramifications you think they have from the dreams you receive.

✮ Intuitive Breakthroughs
Record, along with the date and time, any inklings or bitch vibes you feel. Only time will reveal the truth of your intuition. Make sure you records these findings as well.

⭐ Rules and Creed

No matter what you've been told, no one knows you better than you know yourself. Look long and deep within before writing down your personal philosophy and creed that you currently follow. Write down what it is about your philosophy that you don't like and what you'd like to change. Each time you start a new grimoire they will be different due to your overall growth.

⭐ Classes or Learned Experiences

Our journey along the path of enlightenment will only be as transcendent as we allow it to be. In this section, we have an opportunity to record any information learned in a classroom setting or otherwise.

⭐ Bitch spells, Incantation, and Prayers

In this section you can record bitch spells or affirmations, incantations, prayers, and mantras you've learned via experience, other bitches, or from your coven.

5. Be sure to leave at least one page at the end of your grimoire for additional thoughts or reflection upon your progress.

Bitch Spells and Such

Here's a little-known fact about bitch spells: you've been saying them for years! Throughout the course of our lives, we have picked up a few bitch spells and powerful incantations muttered from the mouths of women who raised us when they thought we weren't listening. Some of these were enlightened, but most probably weren't. In either case we've learned to use this second-hand knowledge for various purposes, such as getting through a destructive relationship without losing our dignity, self-worth, or sanity.

A bitch spell is an incantation that is usually written down in a grimoire or memorized, which can be used for either good or evil. Since enlightened Bitchcraft is about control of self, you will not find spells to cast upon others in this book.

The words alone have little power. For bitch spells to work, they must be accepted by the mind and spirit, and then spoken. Once this occurs, they become powerful incantations that will uplift you and banish common bitch-killers like self-doubt, tainted love affairs, low self-esteem, self-hatred, jealousy, rage, confusion, and arrogance.

The following bitch spells are perfect for recording into your bank of enlightened wisdom, your grimoire. They also give ideas on how to create your own bitch spell.

The Confidence Booster

Trace of shame, trace of fear
'Tis time for you to disappear
From the heart and from the mind
My convictions will spellbind

The Strength Enhancer

Oh, ye bitch within arise, the time has come
For the spine will soon succumb
If much isn't done to overcome
This feeling I have of being pond scum

The Anger Eliminator

Shards of rage, wreckage of fury
Thanks to you, "bitcheresy" cries the bitch trial jury
But not this bitch, not anymore
No longer will you destroy my rapport
'Cause transcendence is all I chose to explore

The Calming of the Inner Gold Digger

Get your own, nuggets and trinkets
It's ill-advised to use your body for profits
Avoid such traps found most common in harlots
A masterful bitch self is the best benefit

The Cave Dweller

Not tonight, O ye troglodyte
Your wicked bitch vibes I will fight
Your motives and actions are trite
For visions of the enlightened bitch are in sight

Stand back ye who try to control me
My powers have been set free
I've looked inside and got an eyeful
On a love that's been hurtful and disrespectful
Under your spell I will no longer suffer
Since your treatment of me has grown tougher and rougher
For now my mind, body, and spirit act as a powerful buffer

To Create Your Own Spell

Spells are created to execute a specific task or perform a duty. In all the spells above, and any you later create, you must discover a need. The next step is to use your mind's eye and picture yourself achieving that goal. Imagine your best self—banishing anything that stands in the way of you manifesting your goal. Now, you must allow yourself to feel what it would be like to accomplish that goal. Lastly, write a two- to twelve-line spell, starting with the problem and ending with the solution.

Remember: to be enlightened, any bitch spell you create cannot and must not be used to control or harm others.

I always wanted to be somebody, but now I realize I should have been more specific.

—*Lily Tomlin*

BITCHCRAFT HIERARCHY

At first glance, all accomplished artisans seem alike. Their mannerisms evoke female power. Their bitch vibrations pulsate with undeniable strength. They all look alike because they all think alike. Yet, things are not always as they appear. There are some basic differences in how they practice their enlightened craft. It doesn't matter if you are sitting in a boardroom or milking cows, each of us, in the matter of Bitchcraft, fits nice and snug into one of the three aspects of the bitch: Queen Bee, Sweet Pea, or Wannabe.

It is a rare bitch that is born a Queen Bee. Most of us start out as either Wannabes or Sweet Peas. Not until we commit ourselves to the craft, focus our energies, and control our actions do we reach Queen Bee status.

It's wise to warn about the purgatory stage between Wannabe and Sweet Pea. A common problem for the neophyte practitioner as she is just getting her feet wet—

in the cauldron, so to speak—is flip-flopping between being a Wannabe and a Sweet Pea. She risks becoming a pitiable schizophrenic bitch. She feels resentment from the times she swallowed her tongue, rather than speaking the truth. Later, she succumbs to overzealous bitching. When this happens she falls into a well of shame. So, when the next ripe situation arises, she falters. She under-bitches one day, only to over-compensate the next.

The Wannabe can also be called a poser. She is able to mimic the qualities or characteristics of an enlightened bitch, but the advanced stage of her craft is only a mirage. Wannabes think they are in control when—in reality—someone or something is controlling them.

Sweet Peas are a bit confused. They don't fake enlightenment like the Wannabe, but when a situation arises that calls for a bitch, they don't always rise to the call. They are too sweet and too kind. They are compassionate, as are all enlightened bitches, but to a fault, resulting in the loss of personal power.

Queen Bees are the queens because their skills in bitchery surpass all others. They are consistent and refined. Their actions and speech are carefully thought out. Queen Bees belong only to themselves; they are never possessed, only self-possessed.

Hierarchy Chart

Queen Bees

☆ focused determination

☆ comfortable with power

☆ strong sense of self

☆ compassionate

☆ wise

☆ seeks power from within

☆ immense strength

☆ seeks change

Sweet Peas

☆ can be passive or proactive on the same issue

☆ seeks external approval

☆ seeks internal approval

☆ careful/overly cautious

☆ straddles the fence

☆ receptive

☆ on the cusp of rebirth

☆ assistant to Queen Bee

Wannabes

☆ a newly established artisan

☆ emotion drives actions

☆ unfocused use of energy

☆ impatient, overreacts frequently

☆ abuses power, superficially uses skills

☆ ignorant of the craft

☆ seeks external approval

☆ assistant to Sweet Pea and Queen Bee

Assess the Enlightened Bitch in You

The following assessment will help you determine your place within the Bitchcraft organizational chart. Be honest. Try not to think too hard. As your schoolteacher once told you, "the first answer is most likely the correct one."

1. **Your ex-husband of six months (whom you still love) informs you of his plan to remarry. Do you:**

    a. Cry and plead with him to remarry you instead.

    b. Make obscene phone calls to his fiancé.

    c. Invite them both over for dinner to check her out.

    d. Give him a piece of your mind about not understanding loyalty, honor, or commitment, and then hang up on him. You acknowledge that you can't control his feelings, and finally accept that you are free to move on with your life and find another love.

2. **Someone ate your lunch out of the refrigerator at work for the fourth time in two weeks. Do you:**

    a. Meekly retreat from the break room and scour the contents of your desk for something—anything—to make the hunger pangs go away.

    b. Leave a note on the refrigerator stating, "I know who you are and I saw what you did!" before complaining loudly and storming out of the break room.

    c. Inform your boss and suggest stricter reprimands.

    d. Douse all your future lunches with habanera peppers in an attempt to weed out the culprit.

3. The love of your life breaks up with you on Thursday so he can party guilt-free for the weekend, only to call Sunday night to make up. Would you:

a. Happily take him back. No questions asked.

b. Take him back but make him suffer first.

c. Ignore his calls until you can exact your revenge.

d. Cut him out of your life, but not before you tell him that your heart doesn't have a revolving door in it and that you deserve better!

4. For reasons beyond your control, you are five minutes away from missing your flight. You are anxiously handing the airline customer service representative your plane ticket when her cell phone rings. "I have to take this call. I've been waiting all day for it," she says before turning her back to you. Do you:

a. Tell her that you don't care about her insipid personal life.

b. Make a scene by loudly telling her how unprofessional she is.

c. Fake a medical condition for immediate, preferential treatment.

d. In a calm yet firm manner, request to speak with her manager immediately.

5. You request a 7 a.m. wake-up call only to get the wake-up call at 4 a.m. Do you:

  a. Scold the hotel desk representative harshly.
  b. Thank them for the call but angrily toss and turn until 7 a.m.
  c. Hang up without saying a word. March to the hotel lobby, tell them to look at the clock, and sarcastically ask if it looks like 7 a.m.
  d. Explain that your wake-up call is for 7 a.m. and you'd like it no earlier than that.

6. Your boss is a close talker. Everyone in the office is afraid to tell him how annoying his behavior is. Do you:

  a. Munch on cloves of garlic every morning until he finds you repulsive.
  b. In the sweetest voice you can muster, tell him how nauseating his breath smells.
  c. Write an anonymous letter to human resources for intervention.
  d. Continuously fill his candy bowl with mints until he asks you why you're being so nice. Then tell him the truth.

Your Score:

For each "a" answer, give yourself 1 point; for each "b" answer, 3 points; for each "c" answer, 5 points; and for each "d" answer, 7 points.

Let's assess your responses. The minimum score is 6 points. The maximum is 42 points. Using the chart below, assess your Bitchcraft level.

> 0 to 10: Re-read chapter one and two before
> proceeding to chapter four
> 11 to 24: Wannabe
> 25 to 36: Sweet Pea
> 37 to 42: Queen Bee

Just because I have my standards, they think I'm a bitch.

—Diana Ross

BITCHCRAFT FOR MOST OCCASIONS

Generally speaking, we use our craft unconsciously to help us get through a difficult or annoying situation. For example, a common cause for the eruption of our bitch volcano—our personal Mount Bitch Helens—is when our significant other turns the channel while we are clearly enthralled. Such mundane occurrences should pass under the radar of an enlightened bitch but nonetheless suddenly, out of nowhere, everyone within a few yards of us starts to feel the growing tremor of our angry bitch vibrations. One might liken our anger to a pool of molten hot lava of interminable depth that comes spewing forth to incinerate everything in our paths!

We've learned that outright bitchiness only gives us strength when consciously and thoughtfully applied. Let's take some anecdotal looks at the following four parts of our lives: family, love, career, and friendship. Within these most significant areas we can channel our bitchiness to good effect as long as we take the enlightened approach of a Queen Bee.

In The Family

Families are like fudge...mostly sweet with a few nuts.
—Anonymous

We should just be honest and open about it—some family members can really make our eyes twitch and jaws clench. They can be selfish, covetous, spiteful, or outright mean. After an episode in their crotchety presence, we are often left wondering if a bad spell has been cast over them. And because they are family, we put up with way more than we should. Below is a common familial situation we may find ourselves in. First we'll examine the reactions of neophyte bitches. Then we'll see how an enlightened Queen Bee would handle it.

Situation

A relative's car is being repaired. You let them borrow your car. Upon their return, your car is missing a headlight and squealing like a banshee.

Automatic Wannabe Response

After an exchange of a few select "incantations," our infuriated poser waits for the relative to collect their car. Working herself up to a frothy lather while muttering,

"I'll show them a bitch," she promptly begins pummeling their car with a hammer. To a Wannabe, two wrongs certainly make right.

Automatic Sweet Pea Response

The Sweet Pea immediately makes excuses for her relative while trying to figure out how she's going to pay for the repairs.

Suggested Enlightened Queen Bee Response

First, she centers her spirit with several deep breaths. Then, she listens to the relative's nonsensical explanation without interrupting. Finally, she unleashes a controlled torrent of obscenity-free reprimand before demanding fiscal compensation. No bitch worth her salt is going to allow herself to be deprived of her broom without a peep, but at the same time, an enlightened bitch knows the difference between a constructive tongue lashing, just retribution, and a violent outburst. All our Wannabe has accomplished with the latter is to invite a lawsuit. Enlightened bitches strive to fix a situation but do so without making matters worse.

For Matters of the Heart

There's just no easy way around it: love can make your bitchery dull. To those on the enlightened path, love has the potential to make the total abandonment of ambitions appear giving. Love by itself is a wonderful thing. It's what some people do in the name of love that causes the most problems. And because we find a person impossible to live without, we throw caution to the wind and place our hearts, dead center, on the dartboard. Below you will find a common statement made by a partner who feels threatened by your enlightened Bitchcraft.

Situation

Your significant other turns to you and says, "You've changed. What happened to that sweet lady I met and fell in love with?"

Automatic Wannabe Response

A volatile situation develops as the Wannabe can sense the threat. She indignantly asks, "What do you mean I've changed? I haven't changed one bit! You're the one who has changed." And her rant goes on until he retracts the statement.

Automatic Sweet Pea Response

Even though she instinctively feels under attack, she ingratiates herself nonetheless. Her feelings of inadequacy overcome her; maybe she isn't as loving as she used to be, has she been hardened by the years? She cuddles up to him, ingratiates herself, and offers a foot massage.

Suggested Enlightened Queen Bee Response

Our enlightened bitch sees right through the question. She remains firm while pointing out how unfair the question is. "All people change. It's a natural part of life," she says. She further makes her point by lovingly patting his protruding gut and saying, "See honey, you've changed, too."

In Your Career

All jobs are easy to the person who doesn't have to do them.

—Holt's Law

It's nearly impossible to avoid developing some kind of mental imbalance from a work environment that distresses you. In some environments it doesn't matter how often you consecrate the area: something or someone will come along to test your bitchery. And because we have to work to live, we suffer little indignities every day. Below is a classic example of office politics designed to break the confident stride of the artisan.

Situation

It's your week to brew coffee. Only, your brew is too strong. A mob of angry villagers have gathered around your desk bearing torches threatening to burn your cubicle to the ground.

Automatic Wannabe Response

The Wannabe will feel embarrassed, defensive, and mildly resentful about having had to make coffee in the first place. Not long into her defense, she begins yelling illogical curses. Wannabes think that this is the way of the bitch. But of course, if you've read this far, you know that such a storm of obscenities will only throw fuel on their already lit torches. Within moments, the Wannabe is strapped to her chair and her cubicle is torched to the ground.

Automatic Sweet Pea Response

The Sweet Pea chokes back tears of embarrassment. After apologizing profusely, she asks, "Do you take your coffee black or do you prefer cream?"

Suggested Enlightened Queen Bee Response

The Queen Bee recognizes immediately that discretion is the better part of valor. She knows it's not enough for a bitch to know when to fight, but also how. Rather than foolishly swinging her bitch wand as a bludgeon, she gently waves it as a conjuring stick. The Queen Bee chooses to cast a spell of beguilement to woo the crowd. She uses her quick wit to subtly disarm them and change the subject. Her beguilement and her smokescreen are effective; she escapes, and what's more, she's persuaded her coworkers to make the coffee for the rest of the week.

In Friendships

Friendship with oneself is all-important because without it one cannot be friends with anyone else in the world.
—Eleanor Roosevelt

Friendships form when you can share knowledge with another. Oftentimes, you can acknowledge a special quality they have worthy of esteem. Or you can recognize yourself in them. Unfortunately, some friendships may not be the knowledge-sharing circle we think they are. And because we may have allowed them to read our grimoire and thereby have access to our innermost thoughts, we begin to quickly discern troglodyte from Queen Bee. Below you will find a common, yet uncomfortable, position many of us find ourselves in.

Situation

Two un-initiated friends arrange an intervention (you're becoming a real bitch lately), under the pretense of dinner and your favorite movie.

Automatic Wannabe Response

Once the true motivation of the get-together becomes clear, the Wannabe starts to get angry. "You're damn right I'm acting like a bitch! Maybe you need to bitch up, too!"

Automatic Sweet Pea Response

The Sweet Pea listens to their heretical banter without defending herself and the path she has chosen. She is slowly becoming swayed by their arguments.

Suggested Enlightened Queen Bee Response

The Queen Bee listens carefully, and even more carefully she punches holes in their argument. Through a series of questions, she gets them to reveal situations when they weren't bitch enough. When was the last time their passive, timid demeanor won them a promotion? In regards to her own bitchery she says, "Ultimately, I don't see the content of your accusations. Is it that I don't meekly sit by while people stomp all over me?" She eventually convinces them that even though she's being a bitch in some ways, she's also being positive. Since she handled the situation in an enlightened manner, she ultimately convinces the friend and her cohorts to take the path less chosen and read this book!

Bitch Traps

Unfortunately, there are some situations in which unpleasantness may arise as a direct result of a bitch pursuing her craft. Watch out for the following traps and try to handle them with your highest order of enlightened Bitchcraft.

Bitch Hunts

When we are identified as belonging to a special group, an anti-social group that chooses not to be in the dark about traditional female roles, we will become suspects. Bitch hunts arise, most often, from a conflict a bitch has with her accuser. Most likely it's someone we know. They've come to expect certain easy-going behaviors from us and when we suddenly stand up, we provoke the hunt.

Bitch Trials

Shame, threats, and fear are used in bitch trials to force suspected bitches to 'fess up and claim their bitchery. Oftentimes, our prosecutors will dig in our personal and professional lives to level their trumped-up charges. These are only a few examples:

⭐ Confirmed bitchery by witnesses, like scorned ex-boyfriends and/or backstabbing friends you've banished from your life.

* Pointing out that your mother took charge of her life and was accused of Bitchcraft.

* Having the intelligence to ask the right questions and the guts to ask the tough ones.

* Preferring to handle your affairs without the assistance or dependence of others.

* Troglodyte naming you to deflect the heat from her.

Bitch-induced Hysteria

People outside of the community will be afraid of us. Under certain circumstances their fear warps into a kind of mild dementia, then hysteria. They have either done something or said something against the artisan in question and therefore fear her bitchery.

Bitcheresy

We must banish all feelings of being offended when one of the enlightened is accused of being a basic, troglodyte bitch. We have to give into the temptation to set the record straight when our bitchy behaviors are misconstrued and stereotyped.

One thing to remember is that people will see only what they choose to see. These persecutions can often be the result of the actions of unenlightened bitches, those who wickedly harm others or have completely devoted themselves to the dark side of the craft.

People are pretty much alike. It's only that our differences are more susceptible to definition than our similarities.

—*Linda Ellerbee*

5

THE COVEN: BITCHES GOT TO STICK TOGETHER

A coven is a group of bitches who get together to convene on things that bother them. Some covens are led by Queen Bees, while others take on a more relaxed organizational structure by allowing members of all levels the opportunity to lead. The number in Bitchcraft covens can be any even number, but try to strive for eight or sixteen for double covens. Meetings should occur regularly enough to keep the momentum of the craft alive and our internal bitch awake, strong, and focused. A suggested amount of time is as little as once a month or as frequent as once a week.

The covenstead, your meeting place, could be anywhere the members feel comfortable, such as a casual restaurant or the home of a coven member.

The structure of Bitchcraft coven meetings can be as laid back as a regular night out with the girls, except with more order and purpose. Or it can be as complex as a board meeting at a Fortune 500 company. In all, it's important that the environment is comfortable for everyone to share and learn the inner workings of enlightened bitchdom.

Telltale Signs of a Strong Bitchs' Coven

- No one bitch is the end-all, be-all of the coven
- Members come from all walks of life
- Small number of bitch wars
- High number of troglodytes getting initiated
- Any dues collected go toward the betterment of the coven and the covendom in which it exists

Bitch Intervention

Bitchcraft interventionism is a delicate matter that must be conducted only by the craftiest of bitches. Since it is one of the most charitable and rewarding things you can do for an unenlightened bitch, it is easy to become overwhelmed with good fellowship. Your heart goes out to the wretched troglodyte as you witness one self-destructive pattern after another. Our misguided cave dweller flips you the bird, all the while rejecting your calm, nonintrusive offer of assistance. Remember, when you conduct a bitch intervention you are attempting to introduce change into another person's life. They may not take kindly to that, but like most enlightened bitches you can see the goal through the emotion. Yet and still, for the sake of fellowship and the future of the craft, we shall make note of their emotions and accept how this could affect the success of the intervention.

Here are the keys to a successful bitch intervention:

1. Two or more enlightened bitches agree that intervention is necessary and has a 50 percent chance of success

2. Create a plan as to what will be said to the cave dweller, the unenlightened, the confused, the abused, etc.

3. Approach her as she is engaging in the unenlightened, self-destructive, or self-deprecating behavior

4. In a respectful tone and manner, inform her of her behavior

Warning: a bitch war can easily erupt if the unenlightened feels "talked down to" by the enlightened. Unless you are mentally prepared for a bitch hunt and the likely consequences of said hunt, then remember how powerful your words and tone can be. You have an aura about you that can be intimidating. It's important to remember this for preparation purposes only; never let fear steer you away from doing something you know you must do.

Warning: avoid approaching a troglodyte for the purpose of an intervention without a plan of action and a coven of highly enlightened bitches to banish her just in case!

Basic Coven Organizational Chart
(customize as needed)

QUEEN BEE
- Conducts bitch interventions
- Enforces articles I-IV

SWEET PEA
- Reviews membership applications
- Enforces the oath of secrecy

WANNABE
- Screens applicants
- Organizes meetings

Official Bitchcraft Covenant

The undersigned, being first accepted by all members of the coven and under the oath of secrecy, does hereby state and certify:

That she is at a high level of emotional maturity and capacity.

That she is fully aware of all risks of potential bitch hunts and subsequent trials inherent in her initiation and participation in enlightened Bitchcraft.

That she is fully able and willing to leave her troglodyte days behind her.

Signature: _____ Date: _____

Printed Name: _____

Witness: _____

Witness: _____

Declaration of Bylaws

Article I. Name & Mission

Section 1. The name of the organization shall be
[Your Coven]

Section 2. We must fearlessly and diligently practice well-thought-out bitchery in all matters of life. We must never suppress the urge to express the truth of our enlightened bitch self. We must believe that we as enlightened, powerful bitches have the control to choose who we are, what we want, and where we are going. We will always give respect where respect is due and expect the same in return.

Article II. Membership

Section 1. Application for voting membership shall be open to any Wannabe, Sweet Pea, or Queen Bee at any point along the path of their enlightenment.

Section 2. Membership shall be granted by majority vote only. All members have the right to deny, forfeit, or terminate membership at any time with just cause.

Article III. Coven Policies and Procedures

Section 1. Any bitch spell that is to be soon used must be approved by the coven committee to make sure it is not going to be used to harm or hurt another. This is to prevent rebel bitches from going about town casting spells on a whim and at random.

Article IV. Other Covens and the Prevention of Bitch Wars

Section 1. Refrain from comparing your coven with another. Avoid turf wars.

Section 2. Never seek to destroy another coven.

Section 3. Seek always to present a united front.

Section 4. The danger of having too many powerful bitches together or in close proximity to each other can incite a bitch war between coven leaders and its members. It is imperative to acknowledge and accept the reality of better bitches and more advanced bitches. Study them and learn from them without losing your individuality and the integrity of your coven.

Bitchcraft Oath of Secrecy

Name of Coven: _____

I , [First Middle Last], do solemnly swear of my own free will and volition to:

1. keep the secrets of the Craft of the Enlightened Bitches;
2. never reveal the location of the covenstead, or any other meeting place to troglodytes, warlocks, incubi, and/or grand wizards;
3. never reveal the identity of any person attending such a meeting, be they fellow bitch or not;
4. never misrepresent the Craft of the Enlightened Bitches as being:
   a. the work of evil, embittered, and conniving women;
   b. remotely connected to male-bashing or men-hating;
   c. in any way connected with narcissism.

Being of sound mind and body, I, having reached the full level of emotional maturity, do swear to the above conditions, recognizing the magnificent powers of karma should I ever step back into the cave of darkness and break this solemn oath.

Signature: _____ Date: _____

Printed Name: _____

Witness: _____

Witness: _____

Pre-initiation Screening Form

Name: _____

Age: _____ Birth date: _____

Assumed Bitchcraft Status
(Queen Bee, Sweet Pea, Wannabe): _____

Date You Exited the Cave: _____

City, State, Zip: _____

Home Phone: _____

Other Phone (indicate which): _____

Why do you want to be an enlightened bitch?
_____

Which bitch do you admire most and why?
_____

If you are partnered, how does your partner feel about enlightened Bitchcraft? _____

Can you host a coven meeting and provide delicious refreshments? _____

Why join a coven and not just practice Bitchcraft alone?
_____

Have you ever been accused of practicing Bitchcraft? If so, what was the evidence? _____

Bitch's Brew

Although you're stronger than most, you can experience moments of weakness and tough times. Relax, you too are only human—super human, but human nonetheless. Use the chart below to help you get through. (Note: please consume brews in moderation.)

Brew Chart

Situation #1:

Expecting a potentially vicious bitch trial

Ailment: Anxious and stressed

Bitch's Brew: Herbal Chamomile Tea

Special Instructions/Precautions: Boil water and steep for four to five minutes.

Expected outcome if used as directed: Calms the mind and body. Relaxes the spirit from repeated persecution. A great antispasmodic.

Situation #2:

You've just learned that the love of your life is nothing more than a philanderer, a common warlock, otherwise unenlightened, and/or evil.

Ailment: Confused and appalled

Bitch's Brew: Herbal Peppermint Tea

Special Instructions/Precautions: Boil water and steep for ten minutes. Sweeten with honey or sugar.

Expected outcome if used as directed: Clears the mind.

Sharpens mental focus and concentration. Soothes headaches commonly caused by warlocks.

Situation #3:

You narrowly escape a bitch hunt with your bitchery intact.

Ailment: Exhausted but jittery

Bitch's Brew: Green tea

Special Instructions/Precautions: Boil water but let it cool before steeping. Steep two to six minutes.

Expected outcome if used as directed: Rests your complex spirit. Encourages your bitch self to let her guard down for a while.

Situation #4:

It's Monday and you're experiencing a mild case of ergophobia.

Ailment: Fear and acrimony set in

Bitch's Brew: Herbal Citrus tea

Special Instructions/Precautions: Boil water and steep, covered, for ten minutes. Sweeten with honey.

Expected outcome if used as directed: Alleviates panic and agitation regarding work. Averts depression due to negative aspects of work.

Situation #5:

Your bitch vibes fluctuated wildly, but you ignored the warning.

Ailment: Overwhelming feeling of regret and lack of aggressive readiness

Bitch's Brew: Earl Grey tea

Special instructions/Precautions: Boil water and steep for four to eight minutes.

Expected outcome if used as directed: Stimulates the mind via increased blood flow. Gives energy for performance.

Sometimes you have to be
a bitch to get things done.

—*Madonna*

6

BITCHCRAFT FOLKLORE: GREAT BITCHES IN HISTORY

Take it from the ladies found in this chapter that trudging along the road to Bitchdom isn't easy. It takes hard work. They were legendary. They remained committed even in the face of great strife. They came from a variety of ethnic and racial backgrounds. They lived hard and loved harder. Most importantly, they made great contributions to society and changed the world with their Bitchcraft. Let's take a brief look at how and why these women made it on the list.

Tiye
(Queen of Kemet), 14th Century BC

Aside from being a super mom, this politically savvy queen achieved the title of "Great Royal Wife." She was given autonomy to meet with top-ranking political leaders who held her in high regard. She did all of this while her husband indulged himself in the palace harem.

Manifested Bitchcraft: She saw her husband running around with harem chicks and didn't lose her focus. She allowed him to build shrines for her and a palace complete with an artificial lake for her to gaze into.

The lesson in this bitchtale: Be focused. We should always have a plan and refrain from letting our emotions pull us off course.

Nefertiti
(Queen of Kemet), 13th Century BC

This gorgeous queen married Tiye's son Amenhotep and had so many enemies that they tried to erase her from existence—figuratively and literally—after she died. She actively ruled alongside her husband for many years, demanding equal respect from all. She understood and fought hard for those around her to understand that women are divinely sacred beings. She assisted her husband in changing how Egypt practiced religion despite priests who felt threatened and fought them for years.

Manifested Bitchcraft: Queen Nefertiti demanded respect as a woman. She understood that as women, we have innate power and wisdom.

The lesson in this bitchtale: Be self-aware. When we know ourselves, we can love ourselves and not fear the real possibility of bitch hunts and trials.

Candace
(Empress of Ethiopia), 300 BC

We have to love a woman who used elephants in battle. She made Alexander crap his pants and think twice about invading Ethiopia, fearing the embarrassing spanking he was sure to get from this woman-led army.

Manifested Bitchcraft: She knew that in any one war, there are two battles: mental and physical. She focused her bitch vibrations and saved the lives of her men.

The lesson in this bitchtale: Be creative. We have to think of ways to get what we want that preserve our livelihoods.

The Trung Sisters
(Vietnam), 40 AD

Around 39–42 AD, when Vietnam was under the Han Dynasty of China, Trung Trac and Trung Nhi inspired and led their nation to rebel against two centuries of Chinese rule. Their army was 80,000 strong with thirty-six of the generals being women (including their own mother). Trung Trac later became their leader after successfully defeating the Chinese.

Manifested Bitchcraft: The Trung sisters realized they had the power to change their world. They weren't intimidated by an army three times the size of theirs.

The lesson in this bitchtale: Be assertive. A lot of the time all it takes to positively change our lives is drive.

Queen Boudicca of the Iceni
(Celtic Tribe), 60 AD

She led a large-scale revolt against the Romans, who succeeded in snatching away her and her daughters' rights to rule their lands after the death of her husband. After they beat the queen for daring to act like a man by governing her own lands, they attacked her daughters. Once her people back in Iceni found out about this, they stood behind her and helped her defeat the Romans in many vengeful battles.

Manifested Bitchcraft: She fought to protect her legal rights and those of her children. She did this even after suffering the humiliation of a public whipping. She focused her bitch vibes and conjured up a few bitch spells to regain what was rightfully hers.

The lesson in this bitchtale: Be undaunted. When you are faced with seemingly insurmountable odds, don't give up. The power to overcome them lies in all of us. We just have to realize it exists, focus our bitch vibes, and execute our plans.

Empress Theodora
(Byzantine Empress, Turkey), 500 AD

A suffering actress first and a take-no-stuff feminist later, Empress Theodora pursued equal rights for women. Thanks to her tenacity, women could own the very property they spent their "sexy" years acquiring. When a mob attempted to overthrow her husband, she told him to "bitch-up" and stay put.

Manifested Bitchcraft: This empress had vision. She saw a better future for women in her empire and seized the opportunity to advance her status in a stifling, oppressive, sexist society.

The lesson in this bitchtale: Be wise. Opportunities to lead and positively change the world are bountiful.

Princess Pin-yang
(Chinese military leader), 600 AD

A masterful artisan if there ever was one. She not only created an army of women soldiers to help her father overthrow his enemies, she won over captured enemies by sharing food. When her father became emperor, he made her a marshal with autonomy previously only given to princes.

Manifested Bitchcraft: Her goal was to become the first female marshal. After boldly going against convention she mustered an army of women soldiers. More for political aspirations than humanitarian convictions, she shared her army's rations with captured enemies.

The lesson in this bitchtale: Be ambitious. We've got to know what we want to get what we want. Think it, live it, and be all about it. Understand how you need to get there.

Amina
(Queen of Zaria) 16th century

Amina came to reign Zazzua after the death of her brother. She accumulated great wealth and power from her battles during the thirty-four years she was in power.

Amina expanded her nation to the largest it had ever been. She ordered "Amina walls" to be built around every military camp. Entire towns started to grow in and around the camps. Soon fortified cities were everywhere.

Manifested Bitchcraft: She convinced her nation that a woman could lead as well as, or even better than, a man. She knew her leadership would be scrutinized, but used that not to stall her progress but feed it.

The lesson in this bitchtale: Be tenacious. The level of our determination decides our outcome. Aim high.

Grace O' Malley
(Irish Pirate), 15th Century

Grace's family motto was "Invincible on Land and Sea." On land, she sought revenge for the murder of her husband and her lover. Go figure. She divorced her second husband before giving birth to their son on her ship while it was being attacked by neighboring pirates. Whew!

Manifested Bitchcraft: She fulfilled her dreams with focused will, passion, and energy.

The lesson in this bitchtale: Be aggressive. Be unstoppable.

Yaa Asantewa—
Queen Mother of Ejisu
(Ashanti), 19th Century

Disgusted by the cowardly fear the chiefs displayed in front of British colonialists, she challenged them by saying, "…if you men of Ashanti will not go forward, then we will. We the women will…we will fight until the last of us falls on the battlefields." It's not clear if the words alone got 'em going or the shame of having women fight their battles, but Yaa Asantewa led the Ashantis in battle against the British.

Manifested Bitchcraft: She felt compelled to stand when none of her leaders would. She banished her fears and inspired those around her to do the same as well.

The lesson in this bitchtale: Be strong. When we are strong, we show others how to be, too.

Don't compromise yourself.
You are all you've got.

—*Janis Joplin*

BITCHCRAFT HAZARDS: TEN MISTAKES TO AVOID

Even the most enlightened of us will slip and fall on the path; the key to success is getting back up. But who likes falling all the time, anyway? Isn't it better to have someone who has already walked the road mark its pitfalls for you? We've already identified one pitfall: practicing without an encyclopedia of effective bitch spells. But this is only one of the typical mistakes made; in this chapter I'll give you ten more. Again, the path to enlightened bitchery won't be complete without a few stumbles, but here are some signposts to keep you from stubbing your toes and ruining your pedicure!

1. Using your powers to control others.
Why shouldn't you do this?

2. Pretending to be something other than what you really are.
Why shouldn't you do this?

3. Suppressing the urge to stand up for what is right.
Why shouldn't you do this?

4. Falling into clichéd roles of bitchiness.
Why should you avoid this?

5. Failing to seize the opportunity for a bitch intervention.
Why shouldn't you do this?

6. Avoid becoming your own worst enemy.
Examples of how you've done this:

7. Letting anger be the sole impetus for your Bitchcraft.
Why shouldn't you do this?

8. Using Bitchcraft for revenge.
Why shouldn't you do this?

9. Taking bitch trials as a personal affront.
Remember that most, if not all, Bitchcraft trials are based upon circumstantial information such as:

- ✯ Being the daughter of a known and feared bitch
- ✯ Having a respected level of intelligence
- ✯ Troglodytes naming you to deflect the heat from themselves

What are other reasons you shouldn't take bitch trials as a personal affront?

10. Failing to seek the assistance of your coven.
Why is failing to seek assistance from your coven so important?

Happiness is that
state of consciousness
which proceeds from
the achievement of
one's values.

—*Ayn Rand*

Remember those glasses that you may have squeamishly raised in chapter one? Well, it's time to raise them once more. Only now, raise them higher and with more confidence than before. By finishing this book, my dear enlightened bitchling, you've not only completed the process of owning your bitchiness, you're now proud to be a bitch since you know what it truly means. Your complex personality will no longer be a source of shame for you. You repel the aspersions cast upon you by the persecutors. Your stride is now self-assured.

In the life you once knew, rarely did happiness and bitchiness go hand in hand. The good news is that now they do! As of this moment, you've taken your life in your hands, owned your bitchery, and developed the skill sets to keep you riding high. The state of perpetual well-being and contentment, the very definition of happiness, is achieved by gradual changes over time.

This book isn't a guarantee you will escape every bitch hunt. Only the skills you've developed will accomplish that. The only thing that stands in your way is you and, okay, maybe a mob or two. But, really, who's afraid of them? Certainly not an enlightened bitch like you!

Ten Powerful Affirmations for a Happier, Well-rounded Artisan!

1. Independence
I seek independence from people, institutions, etc. that gain from my dependence.

2. Self-control
I know how to control myself so that I may see who seeks to control me.

3. Self-love
I know how to really love myself so that I can show others how it's done.

4. Self-worth
I know my worth so that I may see how worthy others are of me.

5. Truth
I know my true self so that I may know when others are being true to me.

6. Confidence
I promote a positive self-image until that's all I see when I look in the mirror. I know how to raise my self-esteem so that I may see when someone is trying to lower it.

7. Ambition
I seek to surpass the limits around me so that I can go where no bitch has gone before.

8. Perpetual state of awakening
I know that every bitch hunt or bitch trial is an opportunity for growth and greater understanding. I'm excited! I finally have an opportunity to find out who my real enemies are.

9. Determination
I know the power of my will so that I may know when the will of another has been broken. I must remember the laws of karma. I will use this knowledge in an enlightened manner.

10. Mental toughness
I know that I am only as good as I think I am. My thoughts will guide me to a reality of my greatest dreams.

Bitchcraft Member Cards

Officially Enlightened Queen Bee

Name:

Dedication Date:

Coven Leader:

Covenstead:

Officially Enlightened Sweet Pea

Name:

Dedication Date:

Coven Leader:

Covenstead:

Officially Enlightened Wannabe

Name:

Dedication Date:

Coven Leader:

Covenstead:

Recommended Theme Music

"11th Hour"—Dionne Farris

"Ain't Gonna Cry No More"—Monica

"Breakaway"—Kelly Clarkson

"Caught Out There"—Kelis

"Didn't Cha Know"—Erykah Badu

"Erased"—Annie Lennox

"Fading Fast"—The Go Go's

"Free Your Mind"—En Vogue

"Free Yourself"—Fantasia

"Girl from the Gutter"—Kina

"Girlfriend"—Pebbles

"Goodbye Earl"—Dixie Chicks (for matters of the heart)

"Higher Ground"—Missy Elliott

"Hit the Freeway"—Toni Braxton

"Hollaback Girl"—Gwen Stefani

"I Decide"—Lindsay Lohan

"I Keep"—Jill Scott

"I Wish I Wasn't"—Heather Headley

"If"—Destiny's Child

"I'm Every Woman"—Chaka Kahn and/or Whitney Houston

"Karma"—Alicia Keys

"Keep Your Head"—Mary J. Blige

"Let Me Show You the Way"—Toni Braxton

"Life Is So Hard"—Eve

"Love Don't Live Here Anymore"—Faith Evans

"Ms. Stress"—Floetry

"My Petition"—Jill Scott

"No More Drama"—Mary J. Blige (great for all occasions)

"No More Rain"—Angie Stone

"Nobody's Fool"—Avril Lavigne

"Respect"—Aretha Franklin

"Strength, Courage and Wisdom"—India Arie

"Superwoman"—Karyn White

"Superwoman"—Vivian Green

"That's Not Me"—Jennifer Lopez

"The Actress Hasn't Learned the Lines" (*Evita*)—Madonna

"Trouble Man"—Angie Stone

"True Colors"—Cyndi Lauper

"Unpretty"—TLC

"Walkaway"—Pink (Matters of the Heart)

"What You Waiting For?"—Gwen Stefani

"Wild Women Don't Have the Blues"—Ida Cox

"Woman in a Man's World"—Chaka Kahn

"You Got Nerve"—Aaliyah

"You Must Be Crazy"—Blu Cantrell

The Art of Bitchcraft Glossary

A

Abitchcadabra. A mystical word that has power for only the initiated. It is believed to have the power to cure low self-esteem, cowardice, and other afflictions.

All mouth and no bitch. An effective put down of a certain kind of over-confident wannabe.

Adept. A master or artisan; an enlightened Bitchcraft practitioner.

B

Banish. To mentally and physically drive away or repel negative energies or people from your personal space and home.

Bitch. Women who challenge the state of traditional gender relationships.

Bitch doctor. A self-esteem healer or a person who promotes the self-actualization of women.

Bitch finder. A person believed to have the power to detect bitches.

Bitch hazel. A non-alcoholic solution such as water and lavender for use in purification rituals.

Bitch hunt. A social campaign launched against strong, ambitious, tenacious, aggressive, and revolutionary women on the pretext of investigating social misdeeds. Used as a cover to harass and undermine women with differing views. If successful, death of spirit, ambition, and sense of self is imminent.

Bitch trial. An informal social examination before an incompetent, often frightened and jealous court of "peers." It is also a test of devotion, patience, and stamina through arduous periods of suffering or persuasion.

Bitch vibes. Good or bad feelings or thoughts radiating from bitches.

Bitch vibrations. An untouchable rhythmic vibe often emanating from bitches.

Bitch wand. An arm-length rod, handcrafted by its owner.

Bitch war. A clash between bitch coven leaders and members.

Bitch's spell. A powerful collection of words used to influence positive change; empowering affirmation.

Bitchcraft. The use of bitchery, especially the use of inner knowledge and the practice of self-fulfillment. An irresistible urge to tell it like it is. Being in a state of continuous, skillful ambition.

Bitcheresy. A belief that disagrees with the enlightened nature of the bitch.

Bitchery. A process of focused will, passion, and energy to effect change in yourself, your environment and around the world.

Bitches' alphabet. The secret writing used among bitches.

Bitch's coven. An organized group of six to eighteen bitches who assemble for ritualistic self-actualization.

Bitch's covenstead. The meeting place for bitches.

Bitch's Sabbath. A noon assembly of bitches to celebrate emancipation of self. A day for rest and relaxation.

Bitchier-than-thou. The art or game of out-bitching a foe.

C

Cauldron. A kettle used in magic rites to restore the self-esteem.

Chalice. A sacred bitch's tool that can be used to represent water or to hold brew for offering.

Circle. The sacred space in which ritual and self-actualization takes place. A group of artisans informally working together.

Cleansing. The act of repelling negative energy from your life.

Conjure. The focused use of mind power, mantras, and affirmations to positively influence life.

Consecration. The act of cleansing and blessing an object or place by charging it with positive energy.

Coven. A society or club of bitches, usually consisting of six to eighteen women.

Covendom. The area in and around the coven.

D

Day of power. A social gathering of bitches.

Dedication. An important ritual in which a bitch devotes herself to the craft and swears never to waver in her focus along the chosen path.

E

Elements. The four basic manifestations of Bitchcraft; the foundation for masterful bitchery.

F

Folklore. Orally transmitted tales of a people, their traditional beliefs, practices, and legends. A study of bitchy behavior.

G

Grand wizard. A wickedly clever, emotionally and physically abusive man.

Grimoire. Highly secret book of rituals, affirmations, training techniques, guidelines, procedures, and declarations of bylaws written with the bitch or coven in mind. Only another bitch can see your book of lights and shadows.

H

Hallucination. A wickedly unrealistic perception of how things really are.

I

Incubus. A man whose mind is overly preoccupied with sex.

Infusion. A potion or brew infused by soaking hot water and herbs together.

J

Journey. The necessary steps to enlightened bitchdom.

Jury. A group formed by bitch hunters to judge and pronounce a verdict on an accused artisan.

K

Karma. An uncontrollable process that guarantees all negative and positive energies a person emits are returned.

L

Law of Responsibility. When one intentionally takes responsibility for the wicked use of Bitchcraft.

M

Mass hysteria. A condition in which a large group of people exhibit extreme anxiety or a set of panic-like symptoms for which there is no physical explanation as a reaction to a skillful Bitchcraft artisan. It can also be a condition caused by negative, war-like Bitchcraft.

N

Neophyte. Beginner Bitchcraft artisan.

O

Outer Circle. A place for neophytes and wannabes until they show enlightened bitchery.

P

Passage. The process of going from one stage to the next.

Purify. To cleanse spiritually and mentally, especially getting rid of any thoughts or feelings that might interfere with positive Bitchcraft.

Q

Queening, The. Celebratory event when the enlightened one becomes a Queen Bee.

R

Rite of passage. Significant event in an artisan's bitchery that indicates a transition from troglodyte to Queen Bee.

S

Social campaign. When the socially dominant members of any collective conspire (for example, by using propaganda) to take a bitch down.

T

Transcendent. Surpassing the usual limits of ordinary experience.

Triple goddess. A unified Goddess that encompasses three aspects: the Wannabes, Sweet Peas, and Queen Bees.

Troglodyte. An unenlightened bitch that hides in caves to avoid defamation, poisons her own cauldron by isolating herself, and works the dark side of the force.

U

Unenlightened. One without true bitch knowledge, conviction, and wisdom.

V

Visualization. The process of conjuring images of masterful bitchery.

W

Warlock. An untrustworthy man; a liar, a philanderer, or a vow breaker.

Y

Yo bitch! An affectionate greeting employed among members of a coven.

Z

Zeal. Eagerness and fervent interest in pursuit of Bitchcraft.

THE ART OF

Bitchcraft

COMPLIMENTARY
TWO-WEEK
GRIMOIRE

Belongs to:

_____

Title of Grimoire:

_____

Date Grimoire began:

_____

Name of Bitchcraft Coven:

_____

My Bitchcraft Mission:

Task	Monday	Tuesday	Wednesday
Practiced at least two acts of enlightened bitchery:			
Impetus for my daily bitch trial: Outcome of my daily bitch trial:			
Identified a troglodyte:			
Identified a warlock, grand wizard, or incubus:			
Experienced karma (specify negative or positive):			
Karmic lesson: Tapped into my bitch vibes:			
Followed the message of my bitch vibes:			

Thursday	Friday	Saturday	Sunday

Week One Reflection

It's time to have a one-on-one with your bitch self. What are her aspirations? How does she feel about finally being released? Chances are she's thrilled! She's unafraid of the sudden exposure. She knows that bitch finders, expecting resistance, are at the ready to tie her to the stake. Still, she's fearless!

Week one goals and aspirations:

Week one record of dreams:

Week one intuitive breakthroughs:

Week one record of personal philosophy:

Week one summary of observations and lessons learned from enlightened Bitchcraft practitioners:

Week one summary of observations and unpleasant lessons learned from a troglodyte:

Week one summary of observations and painful lessons learned from a grand wizard:

Week one summary of observations and disturbing lessons learned from a warlock:

Week one summary of observations and awkward lessons learned from an incubus:

Week One Journal

Have you caused bitch-induced mass hysteria? Note the impetus and the ultimate outcome:

Are you guilty of bitcheresy? If yes, explain:

In what way have you out-bitched a foe? Did you resort to the dark force of your craft to win? What would you do differently?

When you remove the cloak of ignorance and surrender to the urge, it's usually because:

When you fail to surrender to the urge, it's usually because:

Task	Monday	Tuesday	Wednesday
Practiced at least four acts of enlightened bitchery:			
Impetus for my daily bitch trial (note how it's different than last week):			
Outcome of my daily bitch trial:			
Banished a troglodyte:			
Banished a warlock, grand wizard, or incubus:			
Experienced karma (specify negative or positive):			
Karmic lesson:			
Tapped into my bitch vibes:			

Thursday	Friday	Saturday	Sunday

Week Two Reflection

The enlightened bitch in you is out and her ascension is inspiring. The badly informed look on in fearful respect. It's probable that in a week's time the enlightened artisan in you has already caused quite the commotion. To everyone else, the unenlightened especially, she's turned your life upside down. Not that you need much urging at this point in the process, but continue on the path you've chosen. There's so much to gain! It is now time to revisit your aspirations from last week and to breathe new life into them. Please review last week's entries before proceeding.

Week two goals and aspirations:

Week two record of dreams:

Week two intuitive breakthroughs:

Week two record of personal philosophy:

Week two summary of observations and lessons learned from enlightened Bitchcraft practitioners:

Week two summary of observations and unpleasant lessons learned from a troglodyte. If it's the same lessons as last week, why do you think that is? Are you in the way of your own success?

Week two summary of observations and painful lessons learned from a grand wizard. The wizard is losing his hold on you and he's nervous! I don't have to tell you that he'll say anything and he'll do anything to maintain the status quo. However, don't lose a wink of sleep. Leave him quaking in his slick boots. What new lessons have you learned from a grand wizard?

Week two summary of observations and disturbing lessons learned from a warlock. If it's the same lessons as last week, why do you think that is? Are you in the way of your own success?

Week two summary of observations and awkward lessons learned from an incubus. If it's the same lessons as last week, why do you think that is? Are you in the way of your own success?

Week Two Journal

Have you caused bitch-induced mass hysteria?
Note the impetus and the ultimate outcome:

Are you guilty of bitcheresy? If yes, explain:

In what way have you out-bitched a foe? Did you resort to
the dark force of your craft to win? What would you do
differently?

When you remove the cloak of ignorance and surrender
to the urge, it's usually because:

When you fail to surrender to the urge, it's usually
because:

Bitch Spells, Incantations & Mantras

Record any spells, etc. that you find useful and note the level of effectiveness.

Bitch Spells:

Incantations:

Mantras:

Brews & Potions

Record any potions that you find useful and note the level of effectiveness.

For the Mind:

For the Body:

For the Spirit:

Notes

About the Author

Kaaronica Evans-Ware, an enlightened artisan by necessity, is a beauty editor by day and multi-genre writer by night. She was first accused of practicing Bitchcraft seven years ago. Her social calling was, and still is, to embrace her bitch self, hone her craft, and always seize the opportunity to tell it like it really is in her home state of Illinois, and throughout the world.